WINDOWS
VIDEO EDITOR
MADE EASY

Creating Memories the Easy Way

By James Bernstein

Bernstein, James
Windows Video Editor Made Easy
Part of the Windows Made Easy series

For more information on reproducing sections of this book or sales of this book,
go to **www.madeeasybookseries.com**

Contents

Introduction

Thanks to the invention of the smartphone, we can now record all the special moments of our lives, and even the not so special ones as I am sure you have seen if you have ever gone on a website such as YouTube or have an Instagram account! Of course smartphones are not the only device you can use to record video and many people still use video cameras to record things such as weddings, graduations and other special events.

One thing that is pretty common with people who record videos is that many times the video ends up being shown with all the footage that really doesn't need to be seen, or the video ends up not being seen at all because the person doesn't have the means to edit out all the unwanted footage to make a watchable video.

This is where using video editing software comes into play. When you have an easy way to edit and enhance your footage and create something that others would enjoy watching, it makes the editing process fun and rewarding. Plus if you do it right, you can end up with a professional looking video that might even make you some money, or at least get you a bunch of views if you post it online!

Microsoft has included video editing software with Windows for many years which used to be called Windows Movie Maker. Now with Windows 10, they have integrated their video editing software with their Photos app and have renamed it the *Windows Video Editor*.

The goal of this book is to get you comfortable using the Windows Video Editor without confusing and irritating you at the same time. I find that if you explain things like someone is a total beginner, even if they are not, it makes that topic much easier to understand, and that is the way this book was written—so that *anyone* can make sense of the content without feeling lost.

This book will cover a wide variety of topics such as the Editor interface, editing and cropping your video clips, adding audio and images, using effects, exporting your videos and so on. By the time you are done reading this book you will be surprised at how easy it is to make some very professional looking videos using such a simple app.

So, on that note, let's import some videos and work towards winning that Oscar!

Chapter 1 – The Video Editor Interface

Compared to many of the more advanced video editing software that is available such as Adobe Premiere and Final Cut Pro, the Windows Video Editor is fairly simple and easy to get around. This is most likely on purpose because Microsoft assumes that the people who will be using the app will not be professional video editors but rather amateurs or those who just want to create videos from their smartphone footage at home.

 If you are interested in learning more about the more user friendly and much cheaper version of Adobe Premiere then check out my book titled **Premiere Elements Made Easy**. https://www.amazon.com/dp/1676934405

At the end of this book, I will have a link to the video I created during the writing of this book so you can see how all of the edits and customizations look in the final video.

Opening the Video Editor App

The first step in using the Windows Video Editor is to open the app, otherwise you will be going nowhere fast! If you use the Windows *Photos* app to view your videos then you will be familiar with the editor interface since it's part of the Photos app itself for some odd reason.

You might have noticed while in the Photos app watching your video that there was a menu named *Edit & Create* which will allow you to start a new video project right from your current video and include the particular video you are viewing in that new project.

Chapter 1 – The Video Editor Interface

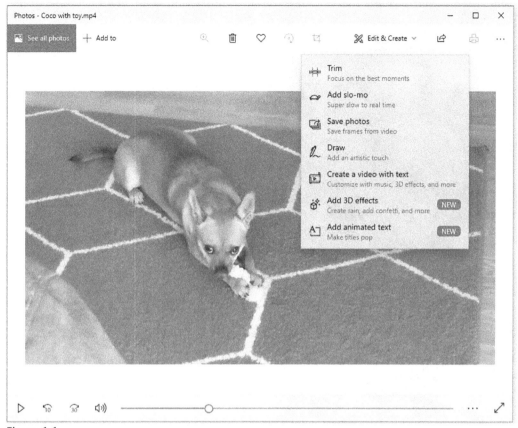

Figure 1.1

If you don't use the Photos app to watch your videos then you can find it on your Windows Start Menu under V for Video Editor. You can also search for it from the search box or Cortana if you use it.

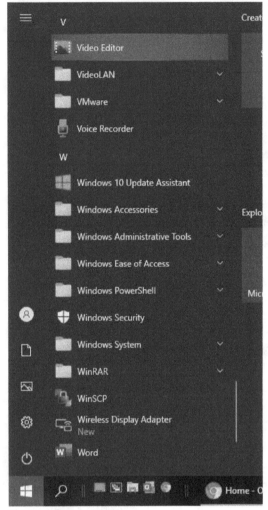

Figure 1.2

Video Editor Interface
Once you open the Video Editor, you will see that it's a very simple interface and if you don't have any existing projects you won't see much except for a button that says *New video project*. If you do have existing projects, you can open them from here and continue to work on them. You might also see a section called *Created for you* that contains a sample video project that Windows put together based on some pictures or videos that you had stored on your hard drive. You can simply ignore this or even delete it if you don't have any use for it.

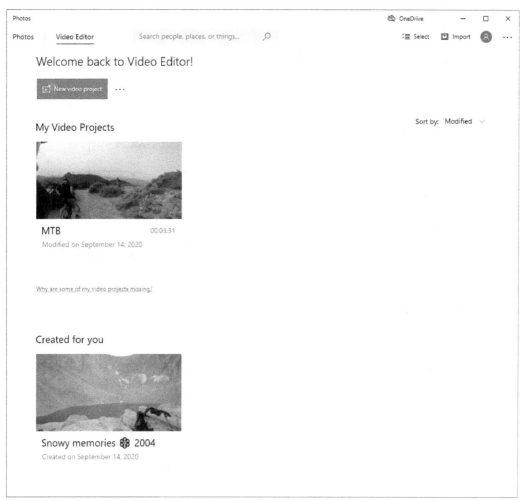

Figure 1.3

Starting a New Project

If you are creating a video from scratch then you will need to click on the *New video project* button to get started with your new project. You will then be prompted to name your new video. I will name mine **Coco & Buddy** since my movie will be based on a couple of dogs named Coco and Buddy.

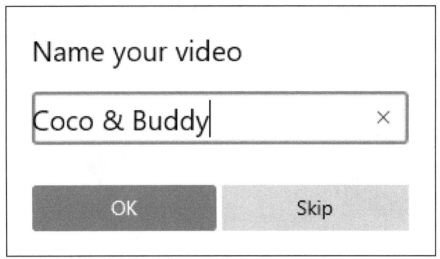

Figure 1.4

As you can see in figure 1.5, when you create a new video project, you won't have much to look at because you will most likely have an empty project library unless you have previously added videos and photos. You can also see that the name of the project is at the top of the screen, and you can change the name by clicking on the pencil icon.

Chapter 1 – The Video Editor Interface

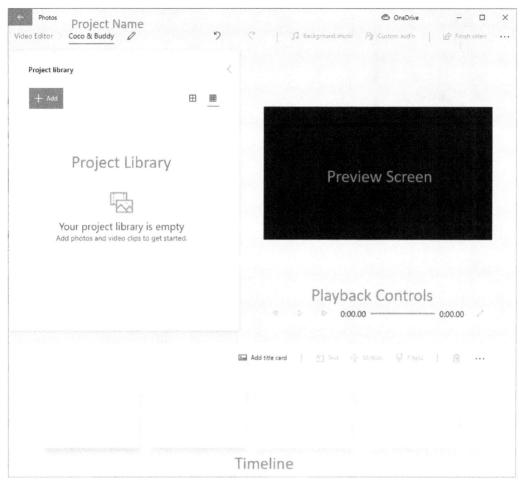

Figure 1.5

The box to the right side of the screen is where you can preview your video as you are working on it and there are playback control buttons underneath as well as a timer section that tells you how long your video clip is. At the very bottom is the timeline (called the storyboard) where you will add your individual videos and pictures that will comprise your entire movie. As you start to add videos to your project and place them on the timeline, things will make much more sense.

You might have noticed that you have the word *OneDrive* at the top of the window. OneDrive is Microsoft's online storage platform and is similar to Dropbox and Google Drive where you can keep your files and also share them with other people.

 If you are interested in learning more about common cloud storage platforms such as OneDrive and Dropbox and how you can use them to backup and share your files then check out my book titled **Cloud Storage Made Easy**.
https://www.amazon.com/dp/1730838359

Chapter 2 – Importing Videos Into Your Project

In order to edit your videos, you will need to first get them into your project so you can then work on them. You might only have one video that you plan on editing, or you may have multiple videos that you want to combine into one movie. You may also have some still images that you want to place within your video as well.

If you will be using multiple video files as I plan on doing for my project you can add them all at once or add them as you go along. And if you find that you have taken some additional video that you wish to add to your final movie, you can add it whenever you need it.

Video File Types and Resolutions

Before I get into how to add your video files to your project, I just wanted to take a moment to discuss some of the more popular video file types and common recording resolutions. The device that you are using to record your videos with will determine the file type and resolution of your recorded videos. Modern video cameras and smartphones will allow you to change the resolution of your videos and often even the type of file used for videos.

Video resolution can be defined as the number of pixels contained in each frame of your video and determines the amount of detail in your video, or how clear the video appears. Video resolution is measured by the number of pixels contained in the standard aspect ratio of 16:9 which is the most common aspect ratio used for TVs and computer monitors.

 You most likely have heard the term 4k video and maybe even 2.7k and 8k. These are higher quality (HD) resolutions and are named for the number of pixels running in a horizontal line across the frame. These resolutions are even higher than 1080p which still looks very clear and sharp.

If you are not sure what type of file you are working with or even your video's resolution then you can find that by looking at the file extension and then the properties of your video file. The file extension is the last three or four characters after the name of the file.

Figure 2.1 shows some files on my computer and as you can see, the first four are MP4 files which are video files and the last four are JPG files which are image files. MP4 file types are very common for video files. You might also run across AVI, WMV, MOV and other types of video files.

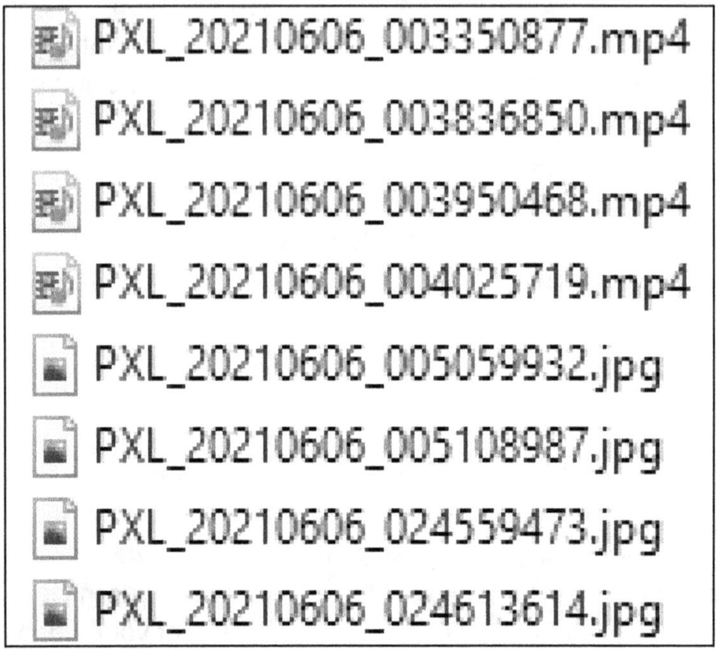

```
PXL_20210606_003350877.mp4
PXL_20210606_003836850.mp4
PXL_20210606_003950468.mp4
PXL_20210606_004025719.mp4
PXL_20210606_005059932.jpg
PXL_20210606_005108987.jpg
PXL_20210606_024559473.jpg
PXL_20210606_024613614.jpg
```

Figure 2.1

To find the resolution of your video file, right click on the file and choose *Properties*. Then go to the *Details* tab and look for the *Frame width* and *Frame height* sections. Figure 2.2 shows that this file has a resolution of 1920x1080 and is known as being a 1080p resolution video. It also shows that this video run length is 26 seconds.

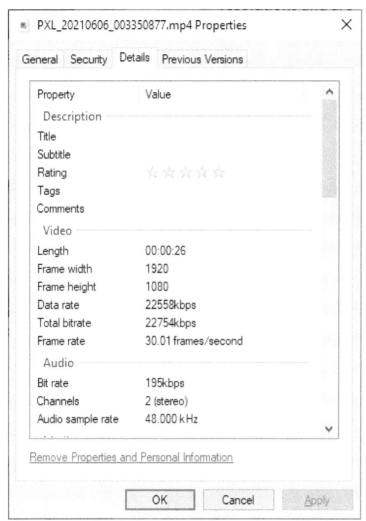

Figure 2.2

Figure 2.3 shows the properties for a GoPro camera video file at 2.7k resolution which is 2704x1520. You can also see that the frame rate for this file is 60 frames per second and the more frames per second, the better the video will be when it comes to capturing movement smoothly.

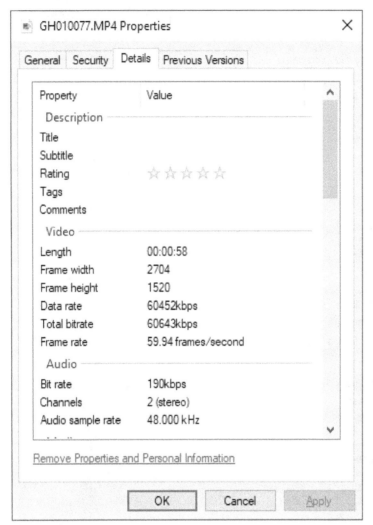
Figure 2.3

The higher the resolution of the file, the larger the file size will be so keep that in mind when importing your video files into your project. This also explains why people run out of space on their smartphones all the time because they take too many high resolution photos and videos!

Downloading Videos From Your Camera\Smartphone

If you are like most people, you use your smartphone as your digital camera and also as your video camera. But then again you might do things the old fashioned way and actually use a real camera! Regardless of which type of device you use to record your videos, you can connect them to your computer usually via a USB cable. The process works in a similar fashion whether it's a smartphone or an actual camera.

There are different makes and models of smartphones, but as of now, it's basically a choice of using an Apple iPhone or a Google Android based smartphone. There are many manufacturers who make Android based phones, and they often customize the interface the way they like, so one manufacturer's phone most likely will look and behave a little differently than another's. iPhones typically stay the same, but Apple adds more features as the newer models come out.

Depending on what model of phone you have, when you connect your smartphone to your computer a few different things might happen. If it's the first time you have connected it to your computer, it may take Windows a while to recognize your phone for the first time. Then you may or may not get a window that pops up showing the folders contained on your phone's internal storage. Some Android phones, for example, make you pull down from the notification area a menu that has connectivity options such as "transfer files" or "charge the phone only".

iPhones will typically pop up a message asking if you want to trust this computer, and you have to confirm before it will let you access the phone's storage from your computer. Once you get into the phone's storage, you will typically want to look for a folder that is called "DCIM", which will have your pictures and video files stored in it. Once you open this folder, you can drag and drop the files onto the desktop of your computer or into another folder of your liking. From there you can add them to your video project. Your video camera will most likely have a similar folder that you can access once you connect it to your computer.

 When adding videos to your project, try and copy them from your camera, USB drive or other external source to your hard drive before importing them into your project. That way you don't risk the video editor not being able to find your files if you unplug your device.

Adding Videos to Your Project
Once you figure out which video and image files you want to use for your project you can then add them to the project so you will be able to access them all from one place.

From the video editor app, you can click on the *Add* button to browse to your file location and then add your videos and pictures from there. Or you can simply drag and drop your files into the Project library itself.

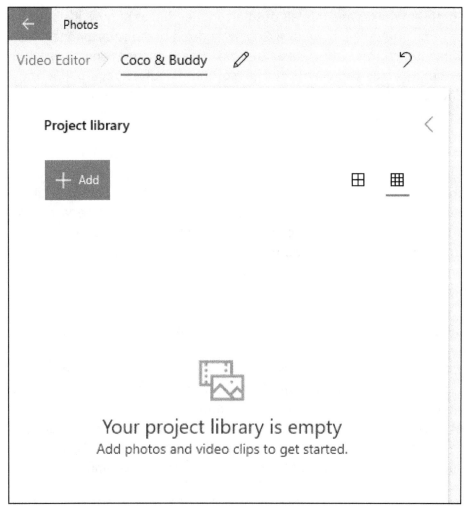

Figure 2.4

I have now dragged a bunch of video and image files into my project, and they are all listed there for me to use for my video if needed. Keep in mind that just because you have these files in your Project library doesn't mean they will be automatically added to your movie project.

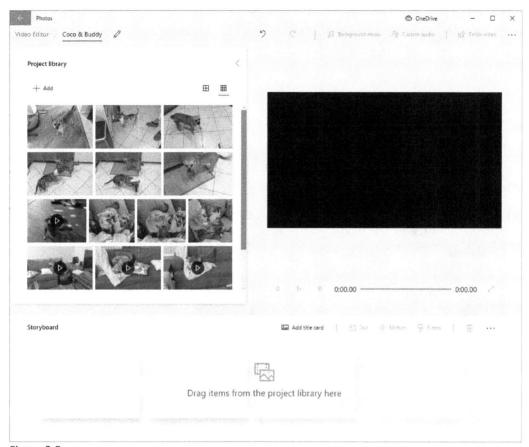

Figure 2.5

You can click on the small and medium view buttons at the top right of the Project library to change how your video thumbnail previews look within your editor.

Figure 2.6

When you click on a particular video or picture, it will place a checkmark in the box at the upper right hand side of the thumbnail and you will then get some additional options at the top of the Project library window.

You will have the option to place the selected file(s) in the storyboard (timeline) or you can also delete them by clicking on the trash can icon. Right clicking on a video will give you the same options.

Figure 2.7

Adding Videos to Your Storyboard (Timeline)

Once you have your videos imported into your Project library, you will then want to start adding them to your storyboard so you can start the editing process. To do so, simply drag them onto the empty white boxes in the storyboard in the order you want them to appear in your video. If you need to change the order of your videos or pictures later on, it's easy to do so don't worry about getting everything perfect the first time. You can drag and drop photos and videos to any location on your storyboard.

Figure 2.8 shows that I have a picture in the first box and a video in the second box on my storyboard. The easiest way to tell is by the icon at the bottom left of each preview. The number next to the icon shows you the duration of each clip. Since pictures are still images, they will be shown for three seconds unless you change the duration manually. The video in the second spot has a duration of 39.84 seconds.

Figure 2.8

Now that I have some footage on my storyboard, I will now be able to see a preview of my movie on the preview screen. I can play and pause the video as needed as well as move back and forth one frame at a time with the left and right arrow buttons. The double arrow icon to the right of the time maker can be clicked on to make the video full screen. You can then press the *Esc* key on your keyboard to go back to the normal view.

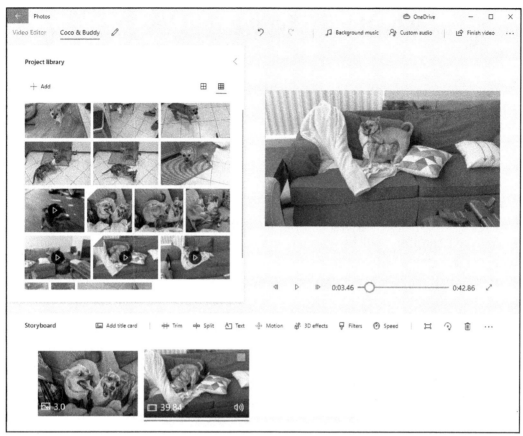

Figure 2.9

To remove a video from the storyboard, I can simply drag it back into the Project library or click on it to select the checkbox and then click on the trash can icon. Don't worry, this won't delete the video from your project but only remove it from the storyboard.

Chapter 3 – Editing Your Videos

Now that you have your videos and pictures imported into your Project library, it's time to start putting them together and making an actual movie out of your various video clips.

You are most likely not going to be using every minute of your imported footage so you will want to do things such as trim down or crop out footage that you don't want in your final movie. Plus you might want to do things such as adjust volume levels and add motion effects to your clips to give your movie a more "polished" look. In this chapter, I will be going over all of the editing options that are available with the Windows Video Editor so you will know everything that can be done to your movie to make it like it was filmed by a professional (sort of).

Storyboard Buttons

When editing your footage you will be utilizing the various buttons that are located above the storyboard that contains all of your video clips and pictures. For the most part, you will have the same options for videos as you do for images, with a few exceptions. Figures 3.1 and 3.2 show the storyboard button options when you select either a picture or a video. The buttons will change as you click on each type of file.

Picture Options

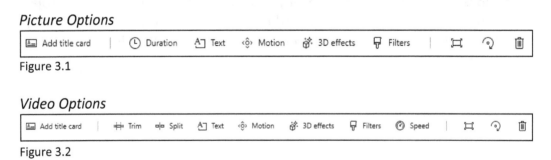

Figure 3.1

Video Options

Figure 3.2

When you are applying something like a filter or adding text to a clip, it will be applied to whichever clip or picture you have selected in the storyboard so make sure you are on the right one before you start making your edits. And if you are looking for something like the speed option but don't see it, the reason will most likely be because you have selected an image rather than a video in your storyboard.

The storyboard buttons should be pretty self explanatory as to what they do but I will be going over each one of them individually as I go through the editing process for my movie. Keep in mind that you don't need to apply every possible feature to your movie just because the option is there.

 Try not to overdo things such as 3D effects, filters and motion transitions because you will end up with a movie that is all about your "special effects" rather than the content of the movie itself. You don't want to have your viewers distracted too much by these types of things.

Adding a Title Card

Title cards are a great way to introduce the subject of your video the same way you would do so for a book. The Windows Video Editor has a bunch of different animated text styles you can use to create your title card in only a few steps.

To add a title card simply click on the first clip in your storyboard and then click on the *Add title card* button and the app will automatically add your title card to the left of the clip you have selected. You can add a title card in other places on your storyboard if you do not want to have it at the very beginning. You can also have multiple title cards in case you wish to use one to separate out a different section of your movie like I will be doing.

Next, you can click on the text style you wish to use and type in your title in the text box at the top right of the screen. Then you can click the *Background* button to change the color of the background if you don't like the color that was provided for you. At the bottom right of the screen you will see a Layout section where you can choose how your text is laid out on the title card.

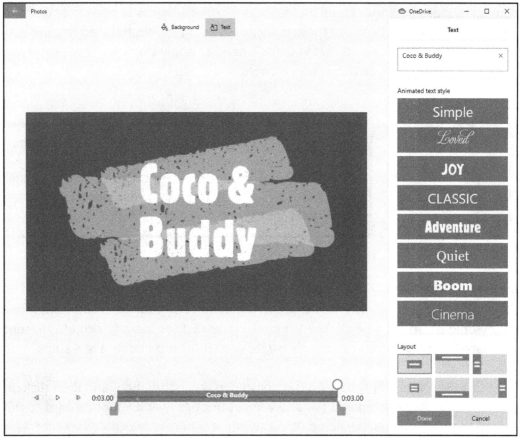

Figure 3.3

At the bottom of the screen is a playback bar that you can use to see how the animation will look which can vary depending on which layout option you use. Once you have everything looking the way you like, click on the *Done* button to have the title card added to your movie. I will also be adding a title card within my movie to introduce each one of the dogs.

Trimming and Splitting Clips
As you add various video clips to your storyboard you will most likely find that you do not want to include the entire clip in your movie and need to either cut off the starting or ending of the video or maybe even cut out the middle. Either one of these edit types is very easy to do and I will be going over both methods.

One thing I want to quickly mention since it's related to the overall length of your video is the duration that still images are shown on the screen. The default duration of a picture that you place in your storyboard is three seconds, but this can easily be changed by clicking on the duration number and choosing another measurement of time, or you can type in your own.

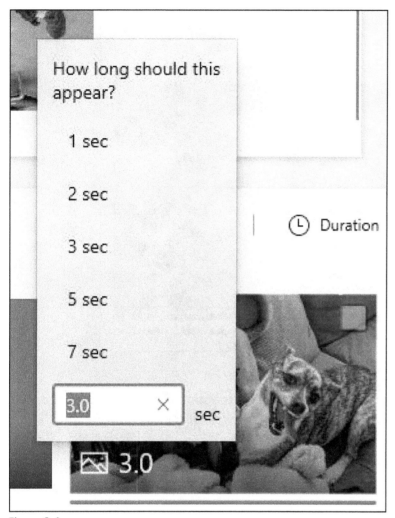

Figure 3.4

Trimming Clips
I have now decided that I want to delete the last part of one of my clips to get rid of some footage I don't need. To do this I will use the Trim feature by selecting the clip I want to trim and then clicking on the *Trim* button. As you can see from figure 3.5, my original video is 39.84 seconds long.

Figure 3.5

Next, I will play the video and pause it right at the spot where I want it to end. This point will be represented by a marker with a circle at the top of it (figure 3.6).

Figure 3.6

Since I am deleting the footage at the end of the clip I will drag the slider from the right side (ending) to the left until I get to the marker that represents when I have paused the video. Then I will click on the *Done* button.

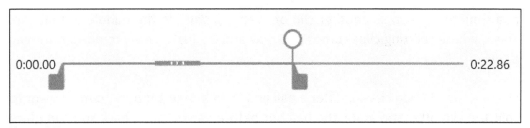

Figure 3.7

Now you can see that my trimmed video is shorter and is only 22.87 seconds long compared to 39.84 seconds before I trimmed it.

Figure 3.8

If you make an edit and realize it was a mistake you can use the Undo button to reverse the action rather than trying to recreate what you had before. The Undo button is the left curving arrow icon at the top of the editor. You can also use the Ctrl-Z keyboard shortcut.

Splitting Clips

You might come across a situation where you have a clip, and you would like to add something such as another clip or even a picture in the middle of that clip. This is where splitting clips comes into play and it's just as easy to do as trimming a clip.

I have a clip of Coco chasing after a ball and then bringing it back to me. I want to split the clip after she grabs the ball but before she brings it back so I can place some still photos in between the two parts of the clip.

To do this, I will select the clip and then click on the *Split* button as seen in figure 3.9.

Figure 3.9

Then I will play the clip up to the part where I want to split it and then pause it. At the top right corner I will be shown the duration for clip one and clip two after it will be split. Figure 3.11 shows a close-up view of this section.

Figure 3.10

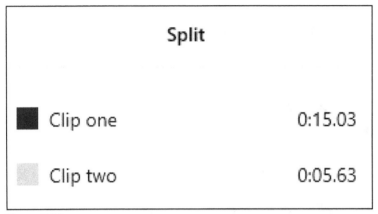

Figure 3.11

When I am ready to split my clip I will click on the *Done* button and then I will have two clips rather than one for that original video and the timestamps for the two clips will match what you saw before I actually split them. The preview for the clips will look the same but don't let that make you think each one is the same.

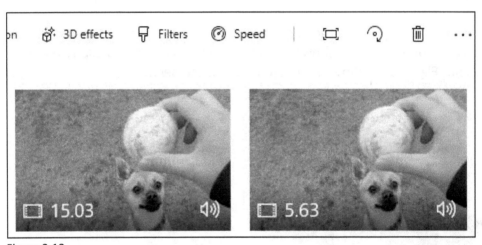

Figure 3.12

I will now trim part of the first clip to get rid of some content I don't want in the video and then drag some pictures in between the two split clips making a slide show type effect between Coco going after the ball and then bringing it back.

Figure 3.13

Removing Black Bars From Photos and Videos

One thing you might run into while editing your video is that you might have some pictures or videos that were taken in portrait mode or in a different resolution than your project and you will end up with some black bars on the left and right side of the photo or video.

Figure 3.14 shows one of my photos that doesn't fit the screen size of my project and therefore displays black bars to fill up the rest of the screen.

Figure 3.14

If you don't like the way this looks and would rather have the entire screen filled with the photo or video then you can crop out the black bars, so they don't show in your project. To do this you will need to select the photo or video and click on the *Remove or show black bars* button and choose *Remove black bars*.

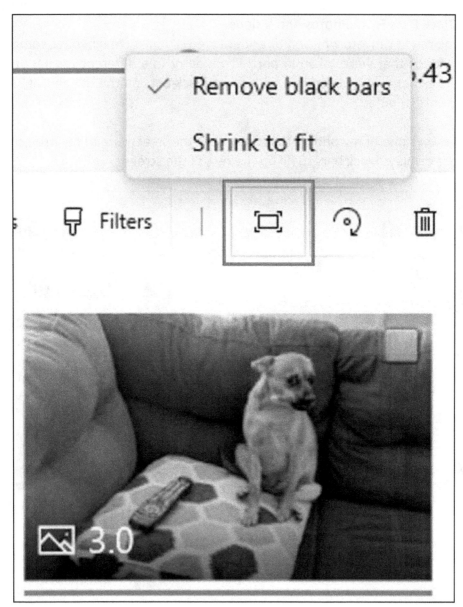

Figure 3.15

As you can see in figure 3.16, the black bars have been removed and my photo takes up the entire screen.

Figure 3.16

The way this feature works is that it actually stretches out your image to fill the screen and remove the black bars. So if you have a picture that has a lot of space on each side (figure 3.17) and you remove the black bars, you might end up cropping out part of your photo or video as seen in figure 3.18.

Figure 3.17

◁ ▷ ▷ 0:42.80 ─────────────────────────────────◯─────────── 0:56.43 ↗

Figure 3.18

Motion Effects

The Windows Video Editor has a feature where you can apply motion effects to your pictures and videos, so they are not just statically switching from one to the next. Even though you can apply motion effects to videos, from my experience it doesn't seem to do much, if anything. But when you apply them to pictures you will be able to see how they work a little better. It's still not the greatest feature since you can't adjust how long the motion effect takes place but it's better than nothing!

To add a motion effect, you will need to select the photo or video clip in your storyboard and then click on the *Motion* button. Figure 3.19 shows all of the types of motion effects you can add to your clips. You will get a limited preview of the effects as you click on each one but the real way to see how it looks is to apply them and then preview your video.

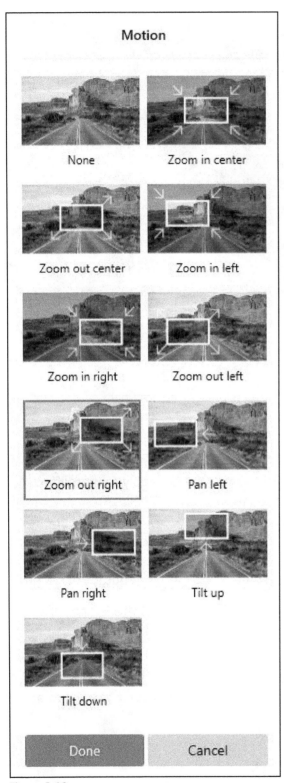

Figure 3.19

38

Inserting Text

You saw how you can insert a Title Card with text earlier in the chapter but sometimes you will want to add text to a photo or even to a video itself. This is an easy process and is similar to creating a Title Card.

To add text to a picture simply select the picture in the storyboard and click on the *Text* button. Then you can choose your font (style) and its position on the picture. At the bottom of the screen you will see a timeline slider where you can determine how long the text stays on the picture. For my picture I will leave it there for the entire five second duration I have set for this picture.

Figure 3.20

To add text to a video, you will do the same process and you can also determine how long the text overlays on top of your video. You can use the slider to set the point where the text will disappear. Or you can have the text stay on for the entire duration of the video clip.

I want my *Let's get ready to rumble* text to continue from my photo into my video and then disappear a few seconds after the video starts playing. So I will use the same font and text layout as I did for my photo and then use the slider to determine how long the text stays on the video.

Figure 3.21

When you click on *Done* and are taken back to the main project window, you will not see your text on top of your photo and video thumbnail previews so you will have to just assume that it's there. You will be able to see your text if you preview your video.

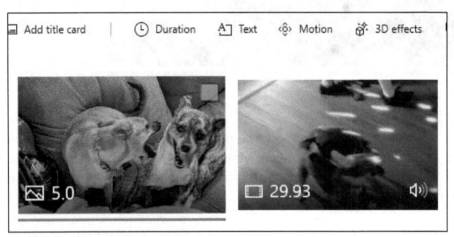

Figure 3.22

When previewing your video, you can start from whichever clip you like rather than playing the entire movie back from the start. Simply click on the clip you wish to start on and then press the play button to have your video start from that point in your project.

Changing the Video Speed
If you happen to be creating a movie with a lot of action you might have the need to create a slow motion scene out of one or more of your clips. Or you might want to speed things up to get past something that might be a little boring yet still important to your overall movie.

To speed up or slow down a video clip, all you need to do is select it and click on the *Speed* button and move the slider to the left to incrementally slow down the video and to the right to speed it up. You should then preview that clip to make sure that it is not too fast or too slow for your liking.

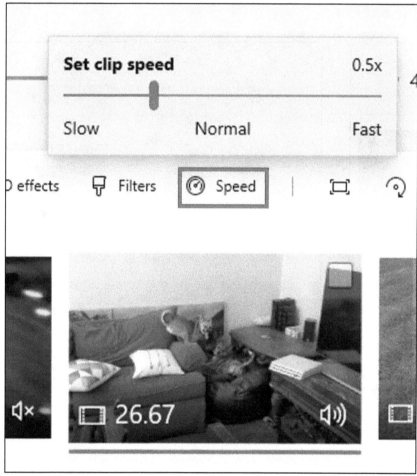

Figure 3.23

If you change your mind and don't want to speed up or slow down your video clip, simply move the slider back to the *Normal* position.

Adding 3D Effects

If you are the type of "director" who likes to add some flair to your videos then you are in luck because the Windows Video Editor comes with some animated effects that you can add to your videos. These effects are not super professional looking but if you are wanting to add something fun to your videos then you can definitely give these a try.

There are two types of effects that you can add to your video clips, and you can actually add them to your photos as well. Once you select a clip you will need to click on the *3D effects* button where you will then be able to select either a standard effect or choose something from the 3D library. If you choose an effect from the 3D library you will then have an option to edit how that effect works after you apply it to your clip.

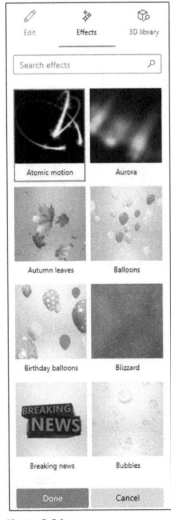

Figure 3.24

First I will add an animated heart effect to one of my pictures of Buddy. Once you place the animation on the picture you can then do things such as resize and rotate the effect. You can also determine how long the effect will stay on the clip and also adjust the volume level of the effect if it has a sound associated with it. You can also drag it around the clip to reposition it as needed.

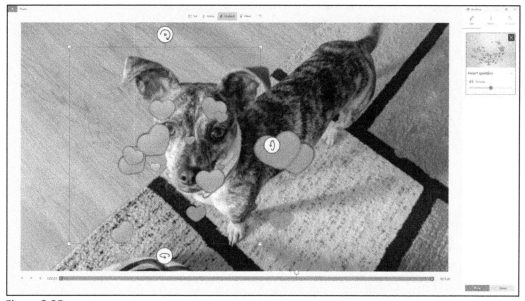

Figure 3.25

For my next effect, I will add two news channel type effects to one of my Coco videos to make it look like it's breaking news. The one that says Live is a still image while the one that says Breaking News is animated and contains sound. You can add multiple effects to a video or photo but just be sure not to get too carried away.

Figure 3.26

For my final example, I will add a 3D effect to one of my videos of Coco and Buddy playing. I will use an animated dog which I will place on the couch next to them. I will then go to the *Edit* section and set the dog to jump and turn as the video is playing. I will also make sure that the effect is applied to the entire video, so it doesn't disappear in the middle of it.

There is also an option that says *Attach to a point*. This can be used to have the animated 3D object follow along with someone or something in your video. You just need to "anchor" the object to the item in your video by clicking on it and then it will try its best to follow along throughout the duration of the clip.

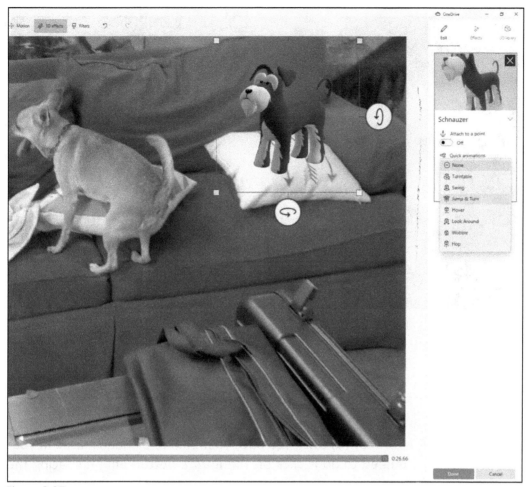

Figure 3.27

Rotating Images and Videos

When using your smartphone to record videos, you might come across a situation where the video rotation doesn't come out correctly compared to how you thought you were recording it. Then when you place the video (or picture) in the storyboard it won't look right.

Figure 3.28

Fortunately, this is an easy fix. Once you have your picture or video placed in your storyboard, all you need to do is click on the *Rotate* button until it's facing the proper direction.

3:37.10 ———————————————————————— O ———— 4:01.33

Add title card | Trim | Split | Text | Motion | 3D effects | Filters | Speed

Figure 3.29

Adding Filters

Filters can be used to alter the appearance of photos and videos such as making them black and white or adding a sepia type of tone to them. They work the same way as adding effects except for the fact that they don't have any motion to them, and they will be applied to the entire clip.

For the sake of making my example really stand out, I will add the Arcade filter to one of my video clips. This filter makes the video look like an old, pixelated video game.

Figure 3.30

Figure 3.31 shows a closer view of all of the various filters that you can apply to your photos or videos.

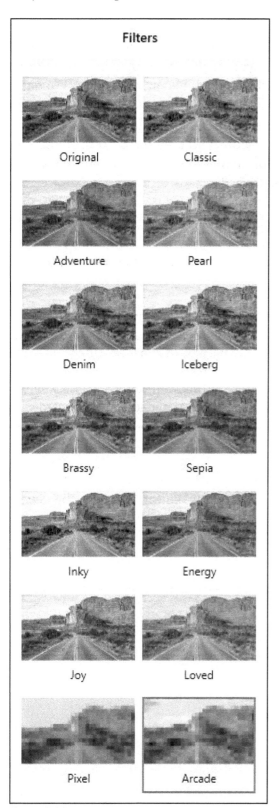

Figure 3.31

Adding Music and Audio

After you get all of your photos and videos inserted into your movie you might realize that it's still lacking something. Or you might notice that there is a lot of background noise or even some other audio you don't want your viewers to hear.

If that is the case, you can add some music or other audio to all or part of your movie to either enhance it or cover up any unwanted audio. Of course you can turn the volume down or even mute it for all of your clips, but I don't know too many people who are into silent movies these days!

With the Windows Video Editor, you have the option to use your own music\audio or add some of their included music in your movie. If you plan on using your own music or audio you will need to have it in a format that can be imported into your project such as an MP3 or WAV file.

 If you plan on using some music from a real artist then you need to be aware of copyright laws and make sure you aren't using your movie in a way that might get you in trouble. Even posting your movie on YouTube with someone else's music can get your audio muted or put your account in jeopardy.

To add some of the music that is provided by the app you can click on the *Background music* button at the top right of the editor to open the *Select background music* dialog box. You can then click on the play button next to each track to hear what it will sound like.

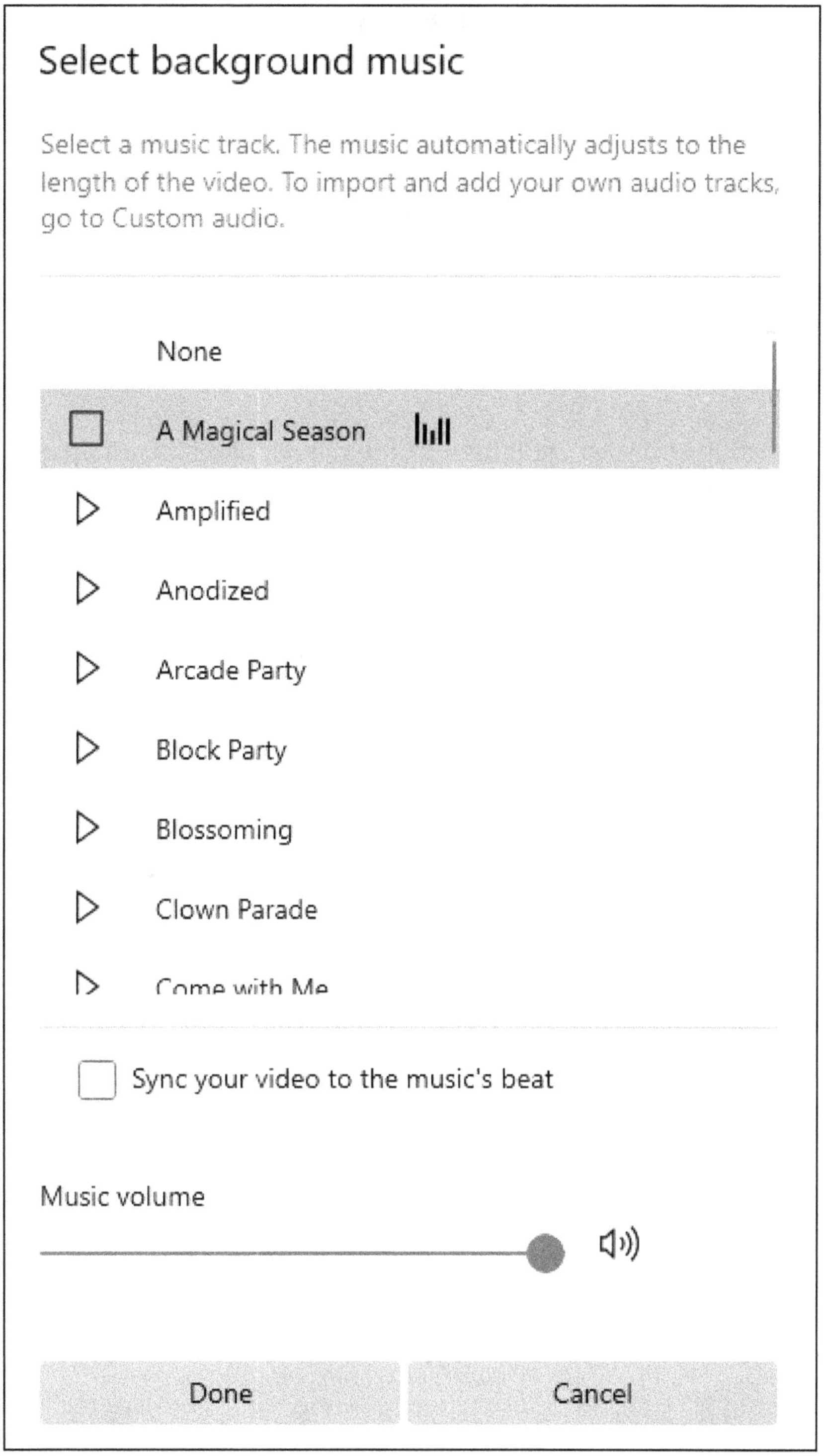

Select background music

Select a music track. The music automatically adjusts to the length of the video. To import and add your own audio tracks, go to Custom audio.

None

☐ A Magical Season   ‖ı‖

▷ Amplified

▷ Anodized

▷ Arcade Party

▷ Block Party

▷ Blossoming

▷ Clown Parade

▷ Come with Me

☐ Sync your video to the music's beat

Music volume

🔊

| Done | Cancel |

Figure 3.32

There is a box that says *Sync your video to the music's beat* which will attempt to adjust the duration of your tracks to match along with the music. You can

51

experiment with this, but I am not a fan of how it works and usually leave it unchecked.

Finally, you can adjust the music volume with the slider and click on the *Done* button to have the music applied to your video. If you find the music is too loud or soft, you can click on Custom audio again to go back in and adjust it. One thing to keep in mind is that if you are using the sync option and add more footage or change the length of how long a picture is displayed, it might throw off the timing of your music and make it end before the movie is over. If that's the case simply go back to Background music and reapply it.

The music will then play for the entire length of the movie, and it does a pretty good job of ending the song properly rather than just stopping in the middle of it. If your video is on the longer side then the music might get a little old since it is sort of repeats itself throughout the movie.

To add your own music or sound effects you can click on the *Custom audio* button and from there click the *Add audio file* button and browse to your music file.

Figure 3.33

You can add more than one file to your movie but will need to make sure that they are not overlapping by arranging the audio tracks so they are next to each other instead.

Figure 3.34

If you are adding a short sound file such as a sound effect to a certain photo or video then make sure you are on that clip before you add it because it will put the time marker at the right place in your project and you can then make sure that your sound clip will play where you want it to play. I will be adding a couple of short sound effect clips to one of my videos and they will play at the same time as the music track that I added to the entire video.

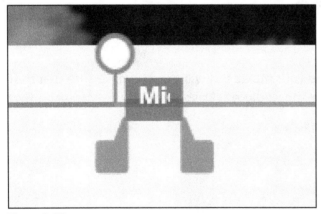

Figure 3.35

If you add your own audio\music you will need to make sure that track volume is not too soft or too loud before adding them to your project because there is no way to adjust their volume within the editor.

Chapter 4 – Exporting Your Video

Once you have your videos, images and sounds all in place and your movie is looking the way you like, you can then export it and share it with the world. Or at least share it with your friends and family.

Before you export your video, you should definitely review the entire movie by watching a preview of it which can be done from the editor itself. Simply click on the first clip in the video and then press the play button to have your movie play from start to finish.

Changing the Aspect Ratio

By default, Windows Video Editor will use the 16:9 aspect ratio which is the most commonly used setting today and is what is known as a "widescreen" aspect ratio. You can think of aspect ratio as the proportional relationship between a video's width and its height. In the past when we had more square monitors and TVs we were using a 4:3 aspect ratio.

The Windows Movie Editor will let you choose either a 16:9 or 4:3 aspect ratio depending on what type of device you are planning on playing your finished movie on. You can even have your video shown in portrait mode (tall) rather than landscape mode (wide). Portrait mode will have a 9:16 and 3:4 setting if you do decide to use this mode.

If you change the mode and your video files don't match then you will end up with black bars either on the sides or the top and bottom of your video. Figure 4.1 shows what happens if I change my project to portrait mode. Since my footage was shot in landscape mode, it won't fit properly into portrait mode, so the editor has to fill the space with black bars.

Figure 4.1

To get to the aspect ratio settings, you will need to click on the ellipsis (...) at the top right of the editor and choose your setting.

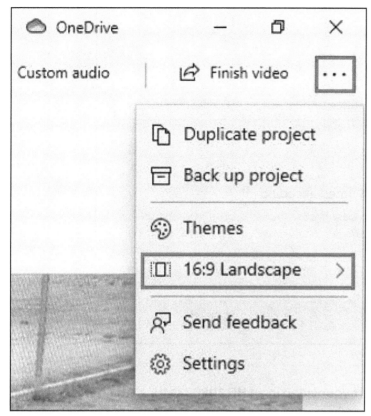

Figure 4.2

You will most likely keep the default setting from when you first started your project but in case you ever want to change it, now you know where it is.

Export Options
When it comes time to export your movie, you have a few options to choose from but overall it's a very easy process and you don't need to be a video expert to do it right.

If everything is looking the way you like and you are ready to go, you can click on the *Finish video* button at the top right of the editor and set the video quality you wish to use. You only have three options to choose from and most of the time you will want to use the *High* setting.

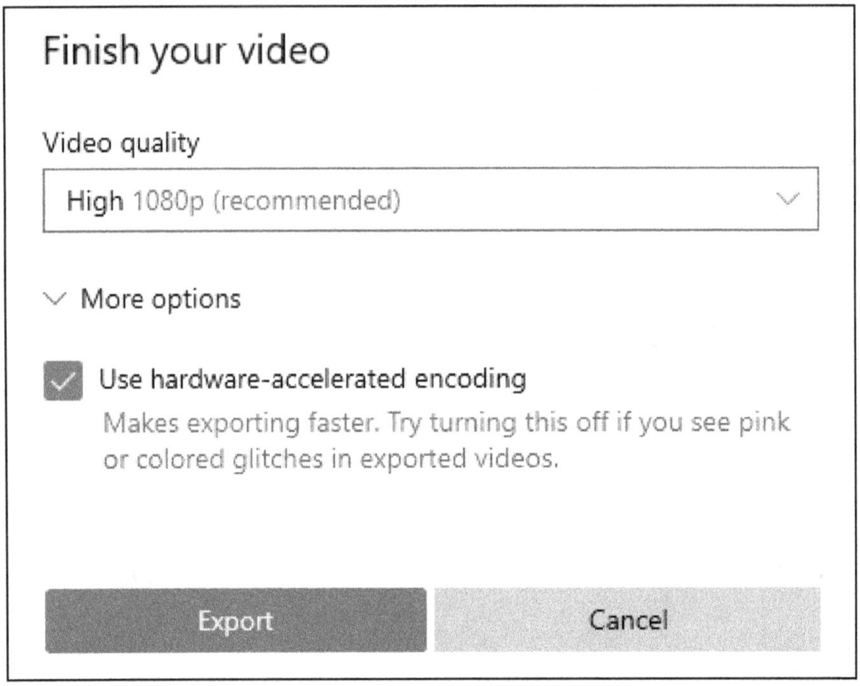

Finish your video

Video quality

High 1080p (recommended)   ⌄

⌄ More options

☑ Use hardware-accelerated encoding
   Makes exporting faster. Try turning this off if you see pink
   or colored glitches in exported videos.

[Export]   [Cancel]

Figure 4.3

The *High* setting will export your video in an HD 1080p setting which will look good on both computers and TVs.

You also have the choice to use the *Medium* setting which is 720p. This resolution is still HD but not as sharp as 1080p but sometimes it's hard to tell them apart depending on what you are watching your video on.

The *Low* setting is 540p and there is no real reason to use this unless you will be streaming it on a very slow connection or storing your movie file on a device that doesn't have much disk space.

These days, 4k and even 8k are more standard video resolutions and look much better than 1080p but as of now, the Windows Video Editor only offers the three resolutions I just discussed.

There is a checkbox that says *Use hardware-accelerated encoding* and I would keep that checked unless you experience any issues in your exported movies after watching them.

Once you have chosen your settings you can click on the *Export* button to begin the export process. You will then be prompted to choose a location on your computer to export the video to. The editor will name the file based on the name of the project, but you can change this if you wish. It will save the file in an MP4 format which is very common for videos and also for sites like YouTube.

You will then see the export process occurring and how long this takes will depend on the length of your movie. You can click the Cancel button at any time to cancel the process.

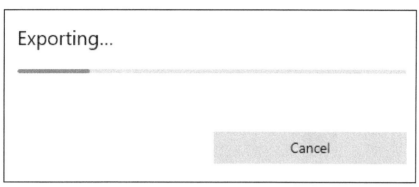

Figure 4.4

When the export process is complete, your finished movie will play automatically so you can sit back and enjoy all of your hard work.

Uploading Your Video to YouTube
Once you have exported your video, you will most likely want to share it with other people so they can see the masterpiece you have created. Your movie file will most likely be too large to email so you will need to use another method to share it. Sure you can burn it on a CD\DVD or copy it to a flash drive but then you will need to make everyone their own copy or keep passing around your media to everyone who wants to see your movie. You can also copy it to a cloud storage account such as Dropbox if you have one.

One of the easiest ways to share a video is to post it on YouTube and then simply share the link to the video with anyone who wishes to see it. YouTube is free and fairly easy to use once you get the hang of it.

The first thing you need to do before being able to use YouTube is to sign up for a Google account. If you already have a Google account then you can just sign in with it on the YouTube website. If you use Gmail then you have a Google account.

If you need to create a Google account simply to go **www.google.com** and click on the *Sign In* button. If you don't already have an account, then you will be prompted to create one (as seen in figure 4.5).

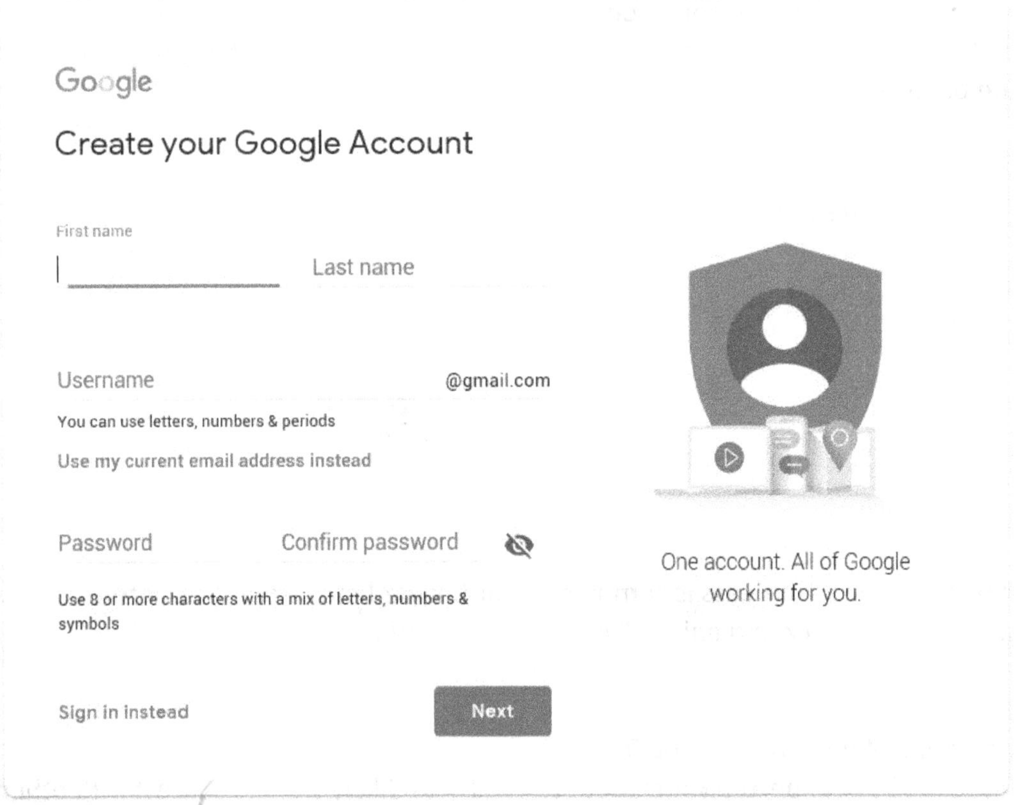

Google

Create your Google Account

First name

Last name

Username   @gmail.com

You can use letters, numbers & periods

Use my current email address instead

Password   Confirm password

Use 8 or more characters with a mix of letters, numbers & symbols

Sign in instead   Next

One account. All of Google working for you.

Figure 4.5

Simply enter your first and last name and choose a username, which will also be used for your Gmail email account ending in @gmail.com. If the username has already been taken, then you will be prompted to enter a new one. Notice that there is an option that says *Use my current email address instead*. This can be done if you do not want a Gmail email address, but still want to create a Google account with your current email address. (I would suggest creating a Gmail email address just to make things easier when using other Google Apps.)

Then you will need to come up with a password that has 8 or more characters and uses letters, numbers, and symbols (such as ! or # for example) and click on *Next*.

After that, you will need to enter your phone number so Google can verify it is really you. It will send you a six digit number via text message that you will have to enter in the next step. Doing this will also tie your phone number to your Google account, which comes in handy for things like password recovery if you forget your password. If you don't have a password you can have Google call you with the code instead of texting it.

Next, you enter a recovery email address (which can also be used for password recovery), as well as your birth date information. The birth date information is used because some Google services have age requirements. The gender information it asks for is optional and is not shown to other Google users. You can also edit your Google account later if you wish to change or add anything.

You may be asked to add your phone number to your account to use for Google services. This is optional, but if you click on the *More options* link you can specify exactly what you want or don't want your phone number to be used for (figure 4.6).

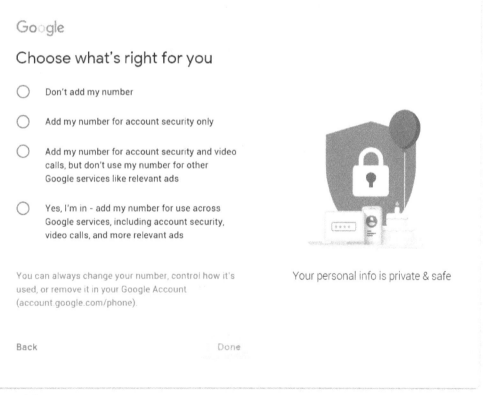

Figure 4.6

If you don't want your number to be used at all, simply click on *Skip*, and you will be brought to the Privacy and Terms agreement, which you can read if you like. To continue, you will need to click on the *I agree* button. Finally, after clicking on

I agree, your account will be created, and you will be logged in automatically. If you are on the Google home page, then you will see your first initial up in the right hand corner. You can go into your settings and edit your profile and add a picture if you like.

 If you have an Android-based smartphone or tablet, then you most likely have a Google account since it is required to have one to download apps on Android devices. You can use this email address and password to sign into YouTube with if you don't want to create a new one.

Once you have your Google account created, simply go to the YouTube website and log in. Next, you will want to click on the *CREATE* button and choose *Upload videos*.

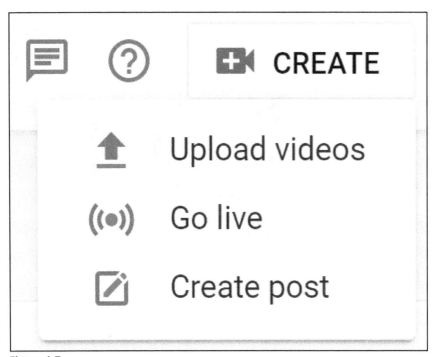

Figure 4.7

Next, you can either click the *SELECT FILES* button to browse to the location of your movie file or you can drag and drop it right into the window as seen in figure 4.8.

Figure 4.8

Next, you will need to add a title and description for your video so people will know what it is about.

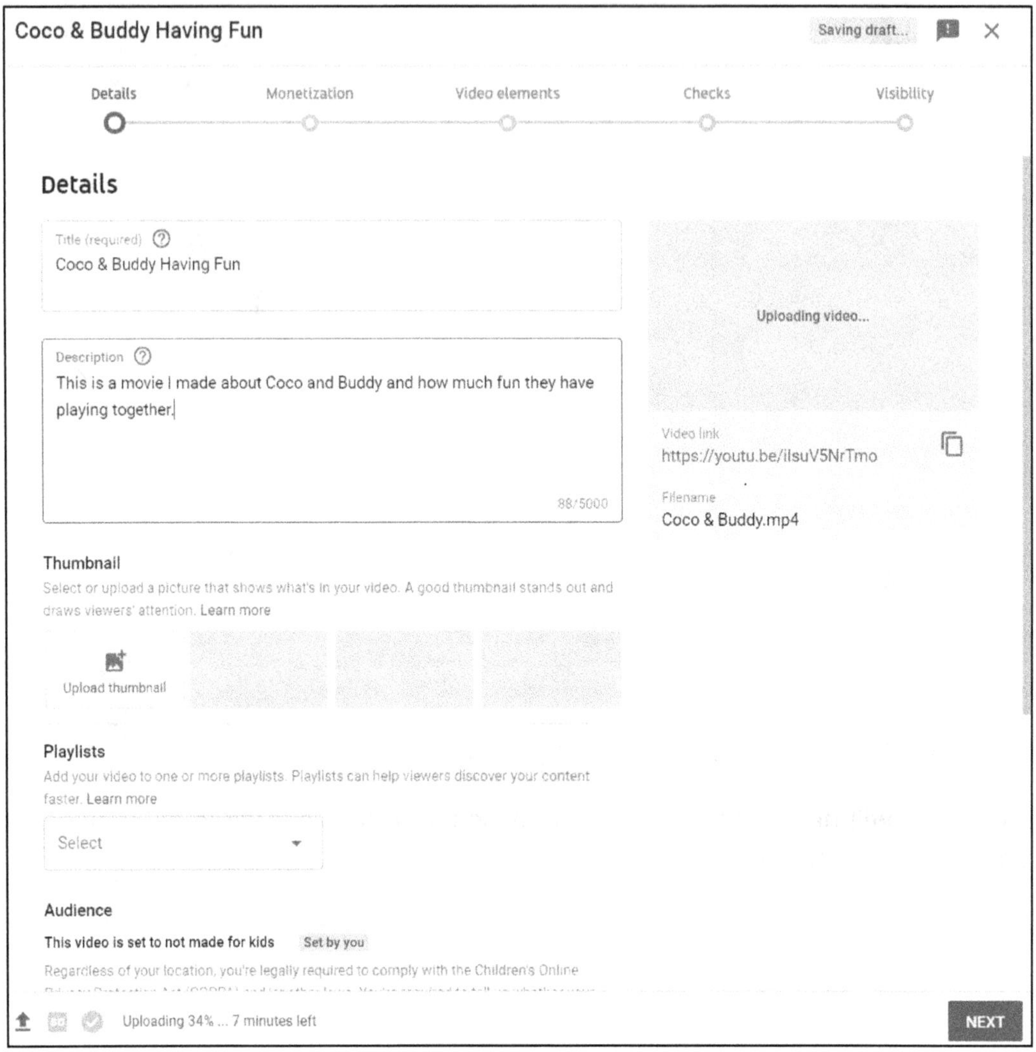

Figure 4.9

Once the video has uploaded it will give you a few thumbnail options which are what appear when your video comes up in search results on YouTube. Once you have a certain number of videos uploaded, they will give you the option to upload your own custom thumbnail.

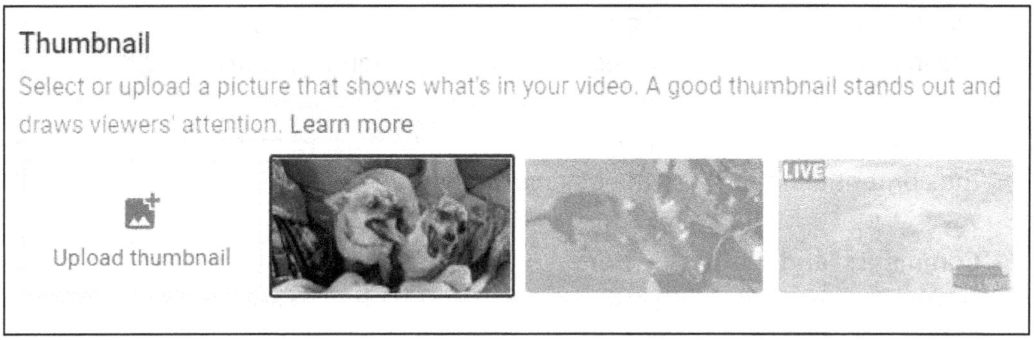

Figure 4.10

There are some additional (and optional) selections you can make from this screen before clicking on the *NEXT* button.

- **Playlist** – You can create playlists to group similar videos together so that your viewers can watch them all one after the other.

- **Audience** – Here you can set whether or not your video is made for kids or has any adult content.

- **Paid Promotion** – If your video contains a product that you are getting paid to show, you can list that information here.

- **Tags** – Tags are used for search purposes so if words or phrases are missing from your title or description that you would like to have associated with your video, you can type them in here.

- **Language and Captions Certification** – If your video contains speech you can set your language options here. The closed captioning section only really applies if your video was on television and used closed captioning.

- **Recording Date and Location** – You can set the recording date here as well as where it was recorded for search purposes.

- **License and Distribution** – Here you should just use the default *Standard YouTube License*. If you want other people to be able to embed your video on their website you can leave the *Allow embedding* checkbox checked. If you have subscribers then you can leave the *Publish to subscriptions feed and notify subscribers* box checked so they will be notified that you have published a new video.

- **Shorts Sampling** – This will allow other YouTube users to sample your video to use in their own video. Uncheck the box if you don't want to allow this.

- **Category** – This is used for search purposes so try and match the category to the content of your video the best you can.

- **Comments and Rating** – Here you can determine if you want to allow comments or not. You can also set it so you will need to approve any comment before it goes live and shows on your video's page.

The *Video elements* section is optional and is used to promote some of your other videos but adding suggested videos at the end of your video from the *Add an end screen* section. The *Add cards* features is also used to add a small popup on your video that viewers can click on to be taken to another one of your videos or one of your playlists.

Video elements
Use cards and an end screen to show viewers related videos, websites, and calls to action. Learn more
Add subtitles
Add an end screen
Promote related content at the end of your video
IMPORT FROM VIDEO
ADD
Add cards
Promote related content during your video
ADD

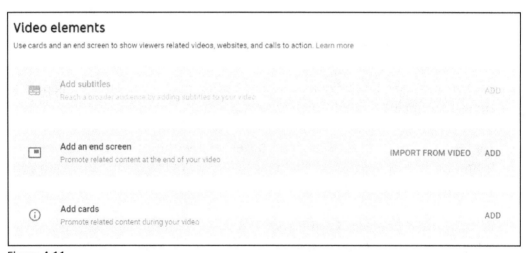

Figure 4.11

YouTube will then check your video for any unlicensed content such as music.

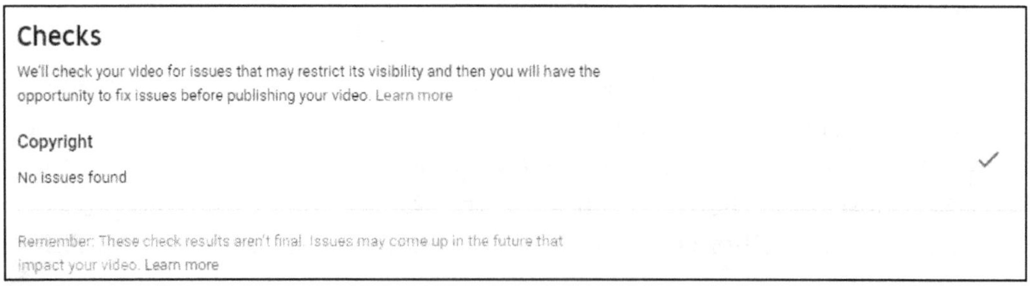

Checks
We'll check your video for issues that may restrict its visibility and then you will have the opportunity to fix issues before publishing your video. Learn more
Copyright
No issues found
Remember: These check results aren't final. Issues may come up in the future that impact your video. Learn more

Figure 4.12

Finally, you can decide if you want your video to be private, unlisted or public. You can also schedule when your video will go live. Once everything looks good, click on the *Publish* button to have your video go live. Unless you scheduled it of course. If you made it private then you will need to email the video link to people to allow them to watch it.

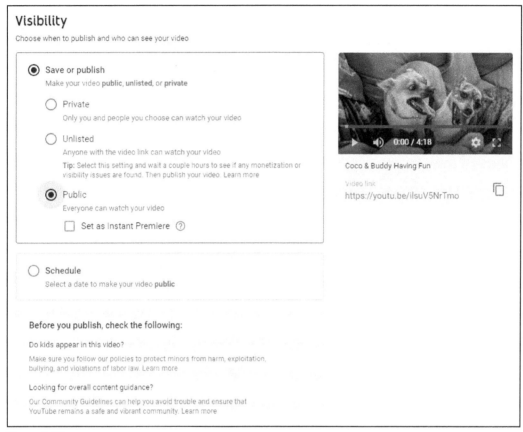

Figure 4.13

You can then go into your *YouTube Studio* and see the stats of your video such as the number of views and so on. Clicking on *Analytics* after checking the box next to your video will give you more detailed viewing information.

Chapter 4 – Exporting Your Video

Figure 4.14

Chapter 5 – Settings and Additional Features

Now that I have covered all you need to know to create your award winning movie, I wanted to take some time to go over some of the settings that you might want to look at for the Video Editor app as well as go over some additional features that you might be interested in learning about.

The Windows Video Editor is a very simple app compared to some of the other software you can use and it's a great alternative for those who just want to create something fun that they can share with other people. But for those who like to dig into every aspect of the software you are using, this chapter is for you.

Video Editor Settings

I mentioned at the beginning of this book that the Video Editor and the Photos app were one in the same and if you are like me, you think that is kind of strange! I wanted to mention this again because when you go to the Video Editor settings you will notice that most of these settings will apply to the Photos app as well.

To get to the settings for the app, you will need to click on the ellipsis at the top right of the screen and then choose *Settings*.

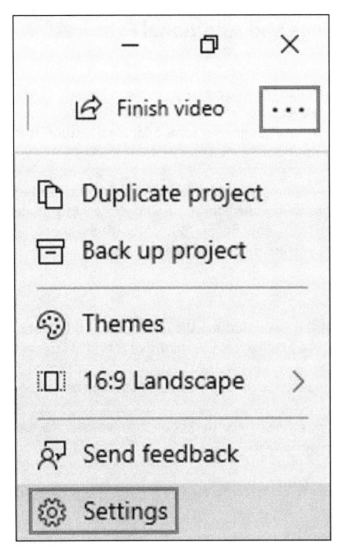

Figure 5.1

Figure 5.2 shows all of the settings in one place, but you will need to scroll down when looking at them yourself. I will now go over the settings that I think are important to know about.

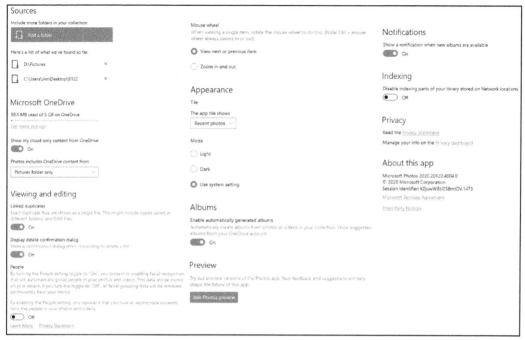

Figure 5.2

- **Sources** – When you are working on a video project, the Video Editor will look for photos and videos in certain locations to make it easier to use them in your project. If you would like to add additional source locations that the app can use, you can do so here.

- **Microsoft OneDrive** – If you are planning on storing and using files from your online OneDrive storage account, you can enable that from here. It should actually be enabled by default. You can also see how much of your OneDrive storage space you are currently using.

- **Albums** – The Windows Video Editor will look at videos you currently have in your collection (sources) and automatically create albums that you can edit to create movies. You can disable this if you don't want the app to automatically create these albums.

- **Video** – I mentioned that you should keep the option to use hardware acceleration enabled when exporting your videos. If doing so is giving you a problem, you can come here to disable it altogether.

Make a Video for Me Option

If you are the type who wants instant results without having to put in a lot of effort then you can try out the *Make a video for me* option to have the Windows Video Editor create a video for you based on the photos and videos you choose. By using this feature, the editor will choose the music and order of your videos and also trim and mix the footage together to add some variety to the finished movie.

To begin simply go out to the main Photos\Video Editor page where you see your projects and click on the ellipsis next to the *New video project* button. From there you will select *Make a video for me.*

Figure 5.3

Next, you will need to select two or more photos or videos to add to your movie from your project library. Finally, you will click on the *Create* button to have your movie created for you but first you will be given an opportunity to name your new video.

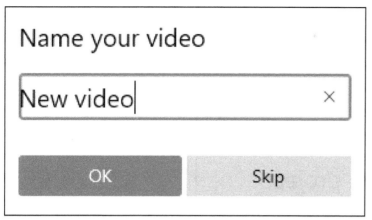

Figure 5.4

I named my video *Auto Created* and after it is completed you can preview the movie and if you want to make changes you can click on *Remix it for me* which will "redesign" your movie with different music and change the order around etc.

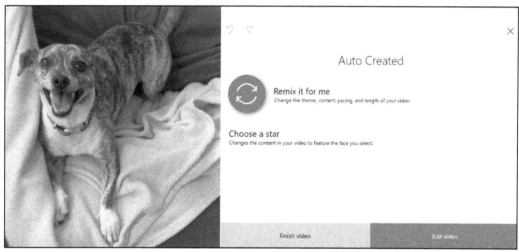

Figure 5.5

You can also click the *Edit video* button to make changes manually or you can click the *Finish video* button to start the export process like you saw in the last chapter.

Themes

If you would like an easy way to have some music, text styles and filters automatically added to your movie project then you can apply one of the built in themes to your project. To get to the theme selection you will once again click on the ellipsis at the top right of the editor and this time choose *Themes*.

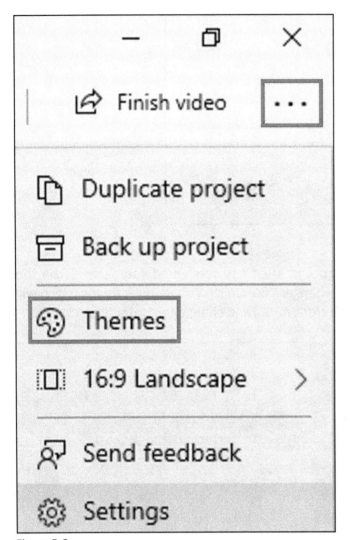

Figure 5.6

You will then be presented with several choices of preconfigured themes. Clicking on each one will show you an example of the music, text styles and filters that come with that theme.

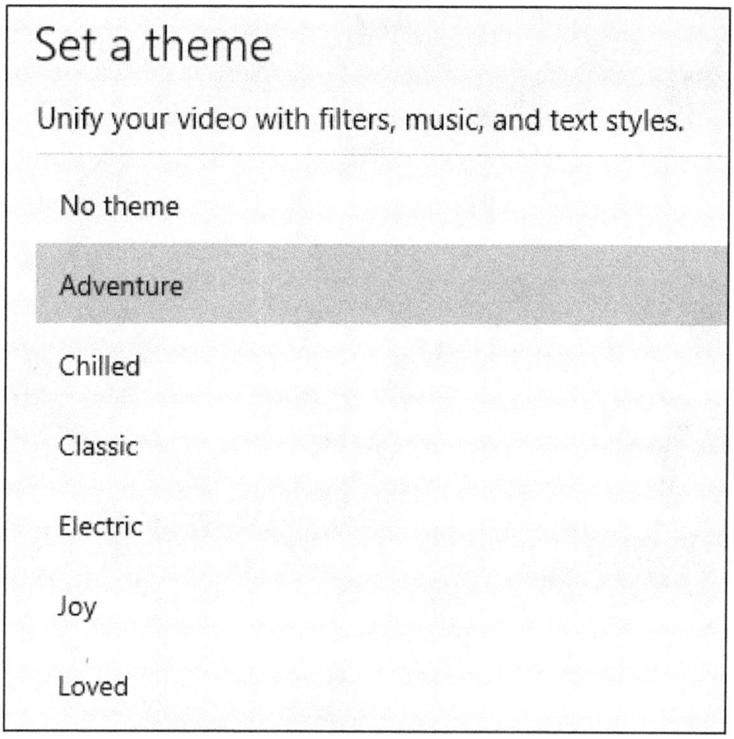

Set a theme

Unify your video with filters, music, and text styles.

No theme

Adventure

Chilled

Classic

Electric

Joy

Loved

Figure 5.7

Figures 5.8 through 5.10 show some examples even though you really can't get the feel for how they look without seeing them in motion.

Amazing colors and light

Figure 5.8

Figure 5.9

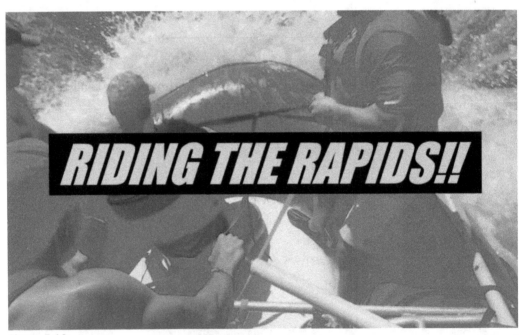

Figure 5.10

Backing Up Your Project

If you have put a lot of effort into your video edits and want to save your work in another location just in case something happens to your original, then you might want to consider performing a project backup. Project backups are easy to do and only take a few minutes.

Once again you will need to go to the ellipsis at the top right of the editor and this time choose *Back up project*. You will then need to select a location on your computer or maybe an external hard drive to save your project. You might even want to create a new folder for this backup file. It will name the backup file after your project, but you can change this if you like.

Figure 5.11

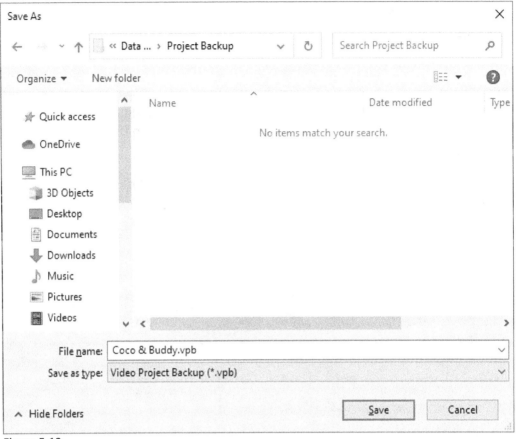

Figure 5.12

 I recommend backing up important files to something like an external hard drive or USB flash drive and then storing it in a fireproof lockbox or maybe take it to a different location such as a friend's house to store it offsite. That way if something horrible happens you will at least still have your files.

After you click the *Save* button, the project backup will begin and how long it takes will depend on how long your project is and how many effects etc. you have within your project.

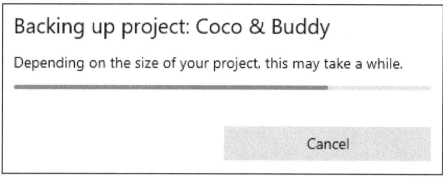

Figure 5.13

You will then be notified when the backup is complete, and it will confirm its location and backup file name.

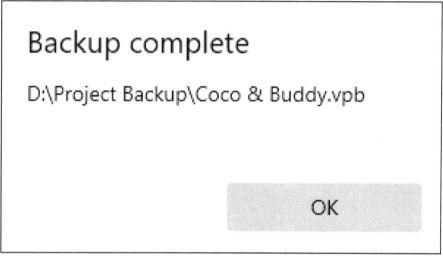

Figure 5.14

The backup will consist of one file and as you can see in figure 5.15, my backup file size is 1.22 GB, and my video is only a few minutes long.

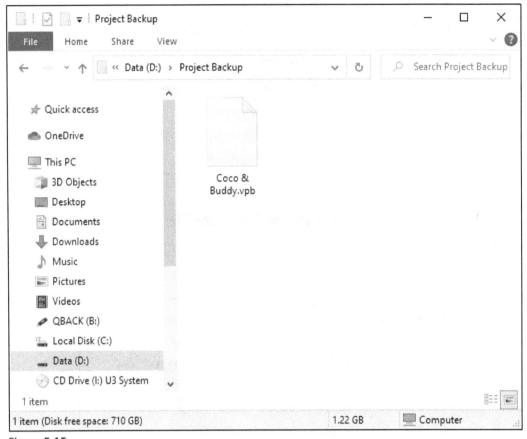

Figure 5.15

Importing a Video Project Backup

Since there is an option to backup your project, it makes sense that there should be a way to restore your project in case the need arises. This can also come in handy if you want to work on your project on a different computer.

If you have a backup of your project and want to import it back to your computer or to a different computer then you will need to go to the main Video Editor screen where you can see all of your projects and click the ellipsis next to *New video project* and this time click on *Import backup*.

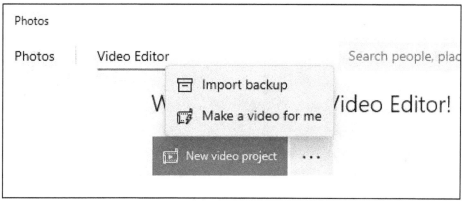

Figure 5.16

Next, you will need to browse to the location of your previously backed up file and select it. Then the import process will begin and will take about as long as the backup did.

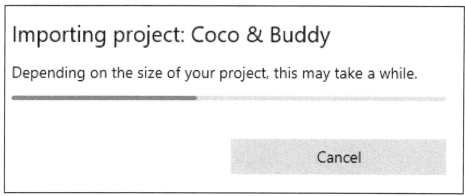

Figure 5.17

The Video Editor app will import it as a copy and will not overwrite your existing copy so be careful which one you continue to edit if you still had your original on your computer. You can then either edit one or both of the projects if you would like to have two different versions for example.

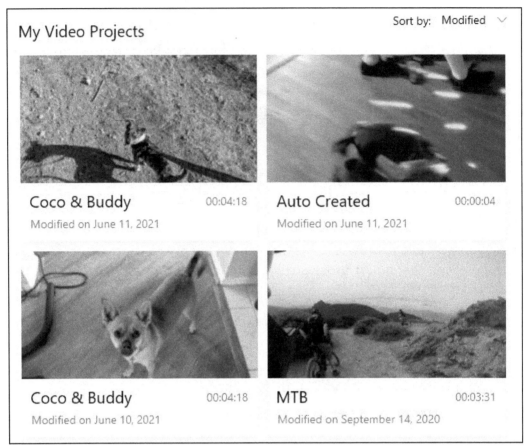

Figure 5.18

Duplicating a Project
I had just mentioned that when you import a project from a backup and still have your original in place that you can then edit either one of them to have two versions.

If you would like to do this but don't want to go through the backup and import process then you can simply duplicate your project, so you have more than one copy of it. Then you can work on each one of them individually to have two different versions.

To duplicate your project you will need to have it open first and then you will go back to the ellipsis at the top right of the editor and this time choose *Duplicate project*.

You can go with the name that the duplication process chooses based on the project name or you can type in your own. I will stick with *Coco & Buddy Copy*.

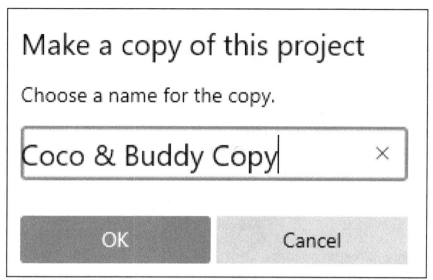

Figure 5.19

The duplication process will only take a minute or less and when it's complete it will take you right into the duplicated project so keep that in mind before you start editing again. You might want to go back out to the main project screen and make sure you see your duplicated project and go back in it from there.

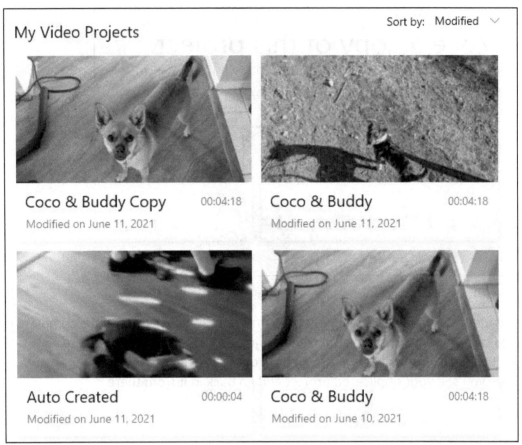

My Video Projects

Sort by: Modified ∨

Coco & Buddy Copy   00:04:18
Modified on June 11, 2021

Coco & Buddy   00:04:18
Modified on June 11, 2021

Auto Created   00:00:04
Modified on June 11, 2021

Coco & Buddy   00:04:18
Modified on June 10, 2021

Figure 5.20

If you need to remove a duplicate copy of your project you can right click on it and choose *Remove*.

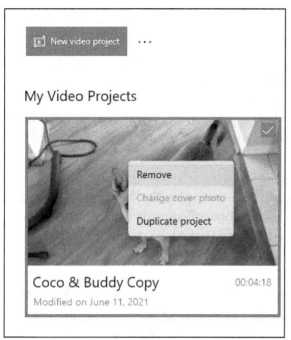

Figure 5.21

Then you will be warned that it will only delete the project and not your photos and videos.

Remove this video project?

We won't delete the photos, video clips, or audio files that are used in this video.

Remove	Cancel

Figure 5.22

Now that my video is complete I will upload it to YouTube, and you can check it out for yourself to see the finished result. I purposely overdid it when it came to effects and filters etc. to show you how they work, and I don't recommend you do the same for your videos!

Here is the link
https://www.youtube.com/watch?v=CIR1X8nmeew

What's Next?

Now that you have read through this book and taken your video editing skills to the next level, you might be wondering what you should do next. Well, that depends on where you want to go. Are you happy with what you have learned, or do you want to further your knowledge with more advanced video editing software to try to see if you can make some even more professional looking movies?

If you do want to expand your knowledge, then you can look for some more advanced books such as my book titled **Premiere Elements Made Easy**, if that's the path you choose to follow. Focus on mastering the basics, and then apply what you have learned when going to more advanced material.

There are many great video resources as well, such as Pluralsight or CBT Nuggets, which offer online subscriptions to training videos of every type imaginable. YouTube is also a great source for instructional videos if you know what to search for.

If you are content in being a proficient Windows Video Editor user that knows more than your friends, then just keep on practicing what you have learned. Don't be afraid to poke around with some of the features that you normally don't use and see if you can figure out what they do without having to research it since learning by doing is the most effective method to gain new skills.

Thanks for reading **Windows Movie Editor Made Easy**. You can also check out the other books in the Made Easy series for additional computer related information and training. You can get more information on my other books on my Computers Made Easy Book Series website.

https://www.madeeasybookseries.com/

You should also check out my computer tips website, as well as follow it on Facebook to find more information on all kinds of computer topics.

www.onlinecomputertips.com
https://www.facebook.com/OnlineComputerTips/

About the Author

James Bernstein has been working with various companies in the IT field since 2000, managing technologies such as SAN and NAS storage, VMware, backups, Windows Servers, Active Directory, DNS, DHCP, Networking, Microsoft Office, Photoshop, Premiere, Exchange, and more.

He has obtained certifications from Microsoft, VMware, CompTIA, ShoreTel, and SNIA, and continues to strive to learn new technologies to further his knowledge on a variety of subjects.

He is also the founder of the website onlinecomputertips.com, which offers its readers valuable information on topics such as Windows, networking, hardware, software, and troubleshooting. James writes much of the content himself and adds new content on a regular basis. The site was started in 2005 and is still going strong today.